Victorian and Edwardian

YACHTING
from old photographs

"ROSABELLE"

1 Frank Beken with his camera in the launch *Rosabelle*
(*Beken*)

Victorian and Edwardian

Yachting

from old photographs

Introduction and commentaries by

ROBERT SIMPER

B.T. BATSFORD LTD

LONDON

By the same Author

Over Snape Bridge
Woodbridge & Beyond
East Coast Sail
Scottish Sail
North East Sail
British Sail

First published 1978
Copyright Robert Simper 1978

Filmset by Servis Filmsetting Ltd, Manchester
Printed in Great Britain
by The Anchor Press, Tiptree, Essex
for the publishers B.T. Batsford Ltd,
4 Fitzhardinge Street, London W1H 0AH

ISBN 0 7134 0914 2

Contents

ACKNOWLEDGEMENTS
I would like to thank the following people for their
generous help in compiling this book. Lady Beryl
Mayhew, Howth Sailing Club, Hilton Matthews,
The Royal North of Ireland Yacht Club, Beken of
Cowes, Miss Gwen Waller, Suffolk Photo Survey,
Radio Times Hulton Picture Library, John
Perryman, Anthea Balmford, Douglas Gurton and
Sea Breezes magazine
R.S.
Ramsholt

The Yachting Scene

Yachting in the eight decades between Queen Victoria's accession to the throne and the first shots of World War I was part of a wealthy and competitive society. The lavish splendour of the larger yachts throughout this period is something which will probably never be seen again. It is also true that many of the shore-born activities of yachting during this period were closely linked with fashionable society. However, all this side of yachting was quickly forgotten once people were afloat. Even if some yacht clubs only admitted certain people, the sea was a great leveller and treated everyone equally.

Yachting was predominantly a sport which men enjoyed most, but just as today some women equally enjoyed going afloat. One owner was Mrs Turner-Farley of London and Falmouth who raced the 36-ton yawl *Nebula* in the handicap class. Deciding that British designers could not produce a fast enough yacht Mrs Turner-Farley commissioned the American Herreshoff, in 1904, to design a craft to beat the reigning British champions. The result was the 52-foot *Sonya*, but this yacht lacked balance and in spite of frequent attention was never a cup winner and Mrs Turner-Farley sold her in 1909.

Another lady owner was Mrs Workman, who had the 23-metre *Nyria*. There were also many married couples who regularly made long passages on their

yachts, but it is true to say that the majority of women were happy to play a spectator role in yachting. It was not until auxiliary engines were introduced that small-boat sailing became really popular. This was only just starting in the Edwardian era.

Throughout the Victorian and Edwardian eras all yachts of any size were sailed by professional crews. They gave employment to many hundreds of inshore fishermen since most of the British fisheries could only be worked in the winter. Men who spent the winter months enduring the dangers and sometimes small returns of longshore fishing looked upon summer yachting as a kind of paid holiday. The great disadvantage was that apart from the skipper most of the yacht hands were hired purely on a seasonal basis so that they lacked security of employment.

In the racing yachts most of the crews were drawn from the Solent, Essex and the Clyde. A yachtmaster recruited his crew from amongst his friends and relations in his home village. There built up a strong tradition of yacht racing in these three areas and racing was made keener by bitter rivalry between them.

A typical yachting village was Tollesbury in Essex. The village stands at the head of a maze of creeks which push through the marshland from the wide River Blackwater. There was no fashionable yacht club anywhere near Tollesbury, nor did many owners and guests ever visit the village. Tollesbury had a fleet of cutter smacks which in winter ranged the Thames Estuary in search of fish or shrimps. But in the spring most smacks were laid up and the men fitted out yachts and sailed them away to race or cruise through much of the summer.

At Tollesbury, as in many other similar villages, yachting was so important to the local economy that boys were prepared for it at school. In the winter two noted yachtmasters, Captain William Frost and Isaac Rice, went to the school in their own time and gave the boys lessons in navigation. On suitable days the schoolmaster instructed older boys in how to fix a position by using a sextant; also further to prepare them for a life at sea older boys were given lessons in knitting, darning and cookery. As well as this most of the boys spent their time playing around the waterfront in small boats and at an early age started going away for trips on the smacks. It is hardly surprising that most of them grew up to be superb small craft sailors. The handling of some of the huge racing schooners and cutters in a fresh breeze under a vast press of canvas and sailing in competition in close company with other yachts called for an exacting standard of seamanship.

On the yachts, especially during long cruises the relationship between the owner's party and the crew was usually informal and happy. Of course being a member of a crew involved the use of a certain amount of tact. A man had to be able to turn a blind eye at what were termed the owner's 'little ways'. Whether this was drink, women or a preoccupation with his health it was no concern of the crew forward.

By present-day standards the crews' wages sound low, but they were actually earning more than men in other similar employment ashore and afloat. Pre-1914 it was usually 26 shillings (£1.30) per week plus keep and a uniform which was kept at the end of the season. During the winter men were taking herring from the sea wearing the uniforms of the King's and other gentlemen's yachts. The really big money was earned on the racing yachts. Because no food could be cooked under racing conditions the men received an extra 2 shillings and 6 pence (15p) allowance a day. Also 10 shillings (50p) starting money, win or lose, and then there was the prize money, £1 for a win, 15 shillings (75p) for a second. The more dangerous jobs such as bowspritman were allowed extra, while the mastheadman, who remained aloft to make certain that the huge jackyard topsail didn't foul up, also got extra payment. At the end of a successful racing season these men returned home very well off. Often towards the end of a good season a yachthand

sent word for a new smack to be completed by the local yard for the winter's fishing. The top racing yachtmasters used to have their own houses built and often they were named after the yacht which won the purchase price. A further symbol of success with Essex racing masters was to drive a pony and trap. That really set them apart from their neighbours.

Both the Solent and the Essex masters loved above all to have fast smacks and work boats built. These they raced in the local regattas held in the autumn after the huge yachts had gone into their winter berths in Southampton or the Essex creeks.

In racing there was another important member of the yachting hierarchy, the sailing master. He was a gentleman, usually of modest means, who understood sailing and more important the intricacies of the racing rules. The professional crew shared the prize money so they always raced, come what may, to win. The sailing master, who often changed as the yacht moved round the coast to different regattas, had local knowledge but was also on hand to advise and even restrain the yachtmaster where racing rules were concerned. Very often the owners were only aboard their craft for a few days every year so that the sailing master often carried out the duties of the owner. In fact the sailing master was the owner's representative, although very often one was aboard even when the owner was there. Many of the better sailing masters were former army officers, possibly because their training made them more suitable to deal with the situations which arose in highly competitive racing. Strangely, officers of the Royal Navy often had great trouble in trying to adjust to the special type of seafaring which comprised yachting. Indeed, there were even frictions with the senior service. Nothing, one yachtsman claimed, was more useless at sea than a wheelbarrow or a Naval officer.

Yachting reflected social habits ashore so that throughout the Victorian and Edwardian periods there were constant wars between the old privileged, landowning, titled aristocracy and the *nouveau riche* who made their money out of industry or merchant ventures and were determined to move into the upper social circles. In America the social order was different, because there top society was mainly comprised of men who had made great wealth by their own initiative and, more important, were respected for having done so.

Towards the end of the century more and more men who had made their fortunes in commerce took to yachting. The established order of landed gentry fought hard, but unsuccessfully, to keep them out. Of course the aristocracy derived their wealth from their estates, which in turn had been created by the skill of their tenant farmers. However the aristocracy liked to believe that they had a kind of divine right to wealth. The new industrial rich were very different people, self-made and ambitious, and they knew that the British way of life always accepted new talent providing it came up through the correct channels. So that a man who made money in cotton manufacture or speculating in shipping or rubber would go to great pains to join the most influential yacht club as a stepping stone to meet the right people and eventually achieve a high-ranking title.

So far as yachting was concerned the influx of great wealth and the driving force of top executives' brains gave excellent sport as well as employment to a great many fishermen. In 1899 members of the Royal Yacht Squadron owned about 150 yachts which gave employment to over 2,000 seamen. Nothing has ever replaced in skill and size the yachts of the Victorian and Edwardian eras which raced in Europe and on the Eastern seaboard of the United States.

The real birth-place of yachting in the British Isles was on the River Thames. There were isolated clubs much older than those on the Thames, but organized racing was developed on the London River. By the mid-nineteenth century even the lower reaches of the Thames were becoming congested with commercial shipping, and the introduction of easy rail travel led yachting to move important events to the South coast, particularly Cowes on the Isle of Wight. Many of the crews, however, still came from Essex and the racing seasons continued to start in the Thames Estuary with regattas at Southend and Harwich. A pattern evolved whereby the Big Class yachts then took part in a regatta at Dover. Yacht racing was then a major spectator sport and the race courses were actually planned so that the crowds on shore received a good view of the huge yachts racing past under a press of white sails. After Dover, the yachts moved to the Solent and then north for the Clyde races. They then went to regattas in Dublin Bay and Cork Harbour and finally returned to Cowes again for the high spot in the year's racing calendar.

Cowes Week at the beginning of August was regarded by many as being the end of the racing season and after it many yachts went off on summer cruises. The keener racing men, however, moved off for a series of regattas in the West Country. Some yachts used to go to the South of France for racing during the winter. At that time the fashionable season on the French Mediterranean was in the winter months as it was considered too hot in the summer. People tended to get their skins tanned by the sun and this was then considered highly undesirable. Most owners were content to lay their yacht up for the winter; the enormous expense of keeping them racing during the summer was enough.

So yachting, although enjoyable for many was also an outlet for social pressures. In fact the famous seasons of coastal regattas in Britain became the prelude to World War I, although few realised this until much later. The German Kaiser had a kind of love-hate relationship with everything British and took to yachting as a way of proving to the proud island race that Germany could better their efforts. The first German yachts were built in Britain and even had British crews. The Kaiser had the full backing of the German industrial entrepreneurs who were, by the opening stages of the twentieth century, challenging British manufactured goods throughout the world and in particular in South America and Africa. If the Kaiser's yacht could win, like the American schooner *America* had at Cowes half a century before, German prestige would receive a boost throughout the world.

Although of course the Germans won many races and were perfectly capable sailors they couldn't quite achieve a knock-out victory over the British yachts. In the end the German industrialists and military ruling party grew weary of trying to dominate the world through the sport of yachting and tried with disastrous results to do it by brute force. The Great War plunged Europe into a series of disasters which brought about many changes, including the hastening of social reform which ended the grand form of yachting which had existed peacefully throughout the Victorian and Edwardian eras.

Germany's other great contribution to the period was perhaps more worthwhile. In 1885 Gottlieb Daimler put the first internal combustion engine car on the road. Seven years later he combined talents with William Steinway, the piano manufacturer, to produce a gasoline outboard engine for boats. The idea crossed the Atlantic and by World War I outboards were commonplace. By 1915 Cameron B. Waterman had manufactured 30,000 units and another American, Evinrude had made advanced technical developments in the making and designing of this type of engine.

For the gentle sport of yachting it was one change after another; they had only just got used to steam yachts. When steam yachts first appeared they were considered rather vulgar, then they became all the rage and in fact many yachting writers around 1890 were expressing fears that steam was going to replace sail and that yacht racing was only going to last for a few more seasons. What actually happened was that it opened up a new type of power yachting and even more people started going afloat. Most of the really wealthy yachtsmen now had huge steam yachts on which they and their guests lived; also large racing cutters to take part in the regattas and small steam launches to tow the racing cutters and generally act as tenders for ferrying between the shore and the yachts.

Most of the races for these huge schooners and cutter yachts were one-day events organized so that the coastal regattas gave the spectators a really worthwhile day out. There were exceptions, such as in 1908 when seven yachts between 130 and 412 tons 'under the patronage of the German Emperor' raced across the North Sea from Bremerhaven to Felixstowe. After Cowes Week and then Ryde Week owners used also to have a Sweepstake Race from the Solent to Weymouth and then they went on to take part in the Western Regattas at Weymouth, Torquay and Dartmouth. However, neither owners nor professional crews liked passage races; the owners preferred a good day's racing followed by the social life ashore, while crews wished to have the yachts at anchor so that they could get a good night's sleep.

Although it was the affairs of the wealthy yachtsmen with their private fleets that fascinated the public and gave an endless source of copy to newspaper men, the vast majority of yachting people were not particularly wealthy and owned quite small craft. These yachting men were doctors, lawyers and shopkeepers who sailed for pleasure, sometimes with a skipper or paid hand, but more often just with their family and friends or anyone they could beguile into enduring the hardships of small boat sailing.

One such yacht which never caught the limelight was the 30-foot sloop *Syren*, built at Woodbridge in 1842 and sailed for over 70 years on the River Deben in Suffolk. The *Syren* was a permanent feature on the little estuary for several generations, yet little is recorded about her. We do know, however, that the *Syren* had a cannon which was used to start races. She also had a paid hand, a one-legged man called 'Peg' Gray. In those days paid hands in small yachts lived forward in the fo'c'sle and also did the cooking there. When the wind fell light at the end of a palmy summer's day, it was the paid hand's place to row the yacht home.

'Peg' Gray was with the Gall family for years looking after the *Syren*. Mr Gall had a chemist's shop in Woodbridge and because of the difficulties of getting out to sea through the dangerous entrance, before engines were introduced, most of the sailing was done in the estuary. Another small 20-foot sailing yacht was kept in the entrance of the River Ore off the Suffolk fishing hamlet of Shingle Street and the sole income of one man and his son was evolved from looking after this yacht and sailing her for the owner in the summer.

The Victorian public were not interested in amateur sailors and their voyages and they were completely overshadowed by the events of Cowes Week and other great social gatherings. Yet the cruises made by these small yachts were great achievements when one considers the limitations of the gaff yachts which had no engines to help them through the difficult parts. When the wind faded these men had to row their yachts and most yacht cruise log books made continual mention of the hours spent toiling away at the heavy sweeps. When Archibald Dickie built the 31-foot gaff yawl *Sheila II* at Tarbert in 1910, rowlock fittings were naturally included in the usual place in the cockpit sides and also long sweeps for rowing. Yet the canoe-sterned *Sheila II* was built to cruise on the West coast of Scotland and in the Irish Sea. Marine engines were already being fitted into yachts, but it was nearly 40 years before they became anything near reliable.

But it was not just the introduction of engines which made the great differences between Victorian and Edwardian small yachts. The Victorian yachts had straight stems and counter sterns while the Edwardians had spoon bows and canoe sterns. The canoe sterns had their origin in the North American Indian birchwood canoe. In Britain the sport of canoeing was directly inspired by Captain John MacGregor, who had the light-decked canoe *Rob Roy* with double-blade paddle, built for him by Searle at Lambeth in 1865. Over the next few years MacGregor travelled thousands of miles in the great rivers of Europe and the publicity he received sparked off a whole new sport, canoeing.

Sailing and paddling canoes was popular from around 1870–1900. Most large cities were on great rivers and young clerical workers and professional men could afford to buy a canoe and paddle away from city life to the nearby rural areas for a break. Sadly, this pastime died out in its original form because most rivers became so commercial that canoeing was no longer a pleasure. New York, for instance, had a thriving canoe club, but its massive harbour became so lined with wharves and piers that there was nowhere for the canoeist to camp. But some men who began in canoes were later able to afford to buy yachts, and, remembering how good their little canoes had been, they incorporated a kind of canoe stern into that generation of yachts.

The quiet order of life was swept away for ever with the outbreak of World War I. The little Woodbridge yacht *Syren* was laid up and over the next few years no one had time to maintain her so she quietly decayed away. Although in 1909 there had been a great outcry in Germany about the Kaiser employing British subjects on his yacht, when the war started there were still two Essex men on the *Meteor*. There were fears for their safety, but the Kaiser gave them safe conduct back to England and a signed photograph of himself. However, before they could leave, both men had to sign a guarantee not to take up arms against the Kaiser. In fact both enlisted in the Royal Navy Reserve as soon as they reached home.

Maritime Photographers

The growth of yachting in the nineteenth century brought prosperity and purpose to many small waterside towns and villages. As well as boosting boatbuilding and other obvious maritime businesses, yachting also created new institutions such as yachting magazines and the new profession of maritime photographer. There was a tremendous demand for maritime subjects, particularly for postcards. In the 1880s photograph books started to gain popularity and this gave a further outlet for commercial photographers. Firms such as Frith & Co of Reigate, Surrey and Valentine & Co of Dundee were sending photographers round the British coast to record any view which was saleable. W. Lawrence of Dublin caught the beauty of many of the tiny ports in Southern Ireland while R. Welsh, the Belfast photographer, took seascapes and was in the habit of 'improving' his works by adding figures. At least some of the negatives taken by these early photographers have survived. The Frith collection belongs to Rothmans, Lawrence photographs are in the National Museum of Ireland, while the Welsh collection are in the Ulster Museum.

The Clyde yielded plenty of material for two well-known photographers' firms. These were J. Adamson & Son of Rothesay, who styled themselves 'artists and photographers', and W. Robertson & Co of Gourock and Glasgow who described themselves as 'high-class portrait photographs'. Both these firms followed the yachts in the summer and also took ship portraits of new commercial ships as they left the Clyde yards. The glass negatives of these firms seem to have been split up by a dealer, but some are known to be in the Ships of the Sea Museum, Savannah.

America also had some very good photographers who specialized largely in yachts. A large portion of the negatives of N.L. Stebbins of Boston, Mass., thanks to the efforts of the Society for the Preservation of New England Antiquities, has been saved at Boston. During his career as a commercial photographer between 1884–1922 Stebbins produced around 25,000 negatives. He travelled to Cowes, the Victorian yachtsman's mecca and took photographs which appeared in his first book *American and English Yachts* which came out in 1887.

The yachts under full sail made superb subjects. There were, however, some extremely good photographers working on the South coast of England and competition stopped their work from stagnating. Very active in yachting photography were W.U. Kirk & Sons of Cowes. The Kirk family lived on the Isle of Wight, but seem to have had a branch at Southsea on the mainland. The Kirk glass negatives are still at Cowes, owned by Roger Smith.

The photographer Debenham was also working at Cowes, but better known were G. West & Son of Southsea and Gosport. The West negatives were later bought by Beken of Cowes and are now integrated into their collection. This firm was started as a chemist's shop by A.E.C. Beken, but it was his son Frank Beken who developed the marine photography side of the business. The backbone of Beken's work was taking ship portraits, either commissioned or on spec and then displayed in the chemist's shop window to catch the owner's eye.

For work afloat Frank Beken had a special camera made for him by a man working at Samuel White's Shipyard. The camera had a handle on either side so that it could be held steady, and the shutter was released by a pressure valve held between the teeth (see photograph No 1). This camera took whole-plate glass negatives and by 1914 the Beken collection numbered about 10,000. Not all of these have survived; some have broken and others, particularly those of crews and guests, were destroyed at one stage because it was believed that no one would ever be interested in them. The firm has been continued by Frank's son, Keith and now by his grandson Kenneth Beken.

The Solent photographers of the fashionable yachting centres could afford to concentrate on yachts because their wealthy clientele created a regular demand. Another type of maritime photographer was Henry Jenkins. He moved to Lowestoft in the late 1890s. This East Anglian port was basically a new Victorian industrial town, with an even newer seaside resort springing up south of the harbour. Henry Jenkins combined the two; the industry was fishing so he went down on to the South Pier and photographed the sailing trawlers and drifters and then sold the prints mainly to holidaymakers to take home. The harbour was linked with the East Anglian Broads so holiday yachting parties also commissioned him to take photographs.

At this stage there were no cameras on the market which were really easy to operate and the general public had to rely on professionals like Henry Jenkins. Even for him photography was not an easy craft. He used to set off for his place on the South Pier with two heavy suitcases: one with camera equipment and the other with a whole load of $11\frac{1}{2} \times 9$ inch glass negatives. If he was required back at the shop near the harbour bridge then his assistant hung a sheet out of the window. Jenkins also bought up the negatives of the previous Lowestoft photographer, Bevan, and there even appears to have been a photographer working in the town as far back as the 1860s. The Jenkins and Bevan negatives lay forgotten for many decades, but the business has been carried on at the same artistic level by Henry's son Ford Jenkins and now his grandson Peter Jenkins. In the mid 1970s the off-shore drilling industry replaced the sailing smacks and Broadland yachting parties.

Another collection of Edwardian glass negatives which lay forgotten for decades belonged to the Woodbridge chemist and photographer Welton. After his death the shop changed hands and the negatives were left in an upstairs room at the back. They stayed there for about 50 years and eventually their weight caused the floor to sag badly and the whole collection would have been destroyed if Robert Pratt had not put considerable effort and taken some risk in rescuing the better negatives.

The Dover photographer Amos (1873–1942) was decidedly eccentric, but he loved sailing ships of every type and devoted his life to capturing pictorial records of them. Often the Dover pilots came across Amos alone, miles out to sea, in his tiny dory in bad weather, hoping to catch some passing ship. Being a Quaker, his religious beliefs stopped him from working on Sundays. If a particular ship that he wanted to record passed on a Sunday, Amos stood on the beach, a very unhappy man. Amos's father had been a pioneer in photography and was also rather eccentric as he used to dress young Amos up in medieval costume every Sunday. No one used Amos's forename. His postcards were usually signed Amos & Amos, but also sometimes G.T. Amos or E.G.T. Amos. The Dover boatmen knew him as Lew, but his sister called him Hugh. None of this worried Amos as he lived in his own dream world.

Amos didn't bother to adopt new photographic techniques; he used the same old mahogany box camera all his life. In bad weather he would wrap his jacket round his camera at sea and get wet himself. One of his postcards depicts an elderly American called Drake who had sailed from San Francisco in a boat that he had built himself. This American was later wrecked on the Dutch coast, but he returned to Dover and stayed at Amos's shop which was packed with ship and yacht photographs.

When Amos was out in his boat his sister sat on the beach wrapped up in huge shawls, even in the worst winter, watching for his return. One of Amos' great delights was to wander along the seashore naked, and later in life his tall very thin figure, brown as a berry, was regarded as being one of the strange sights of the district. The Amos's had very little idea of how to run a business and in later life they lived in great deprivation. In World War II Amos's shop received a direct hit from a German gun sited on the French coast. Most of the huge collection of maritime negatives were smashed. Later a dealer split up the remaining ones and some of these have been accumulated by the National Maritime Museum, Greenwich. George Osbon, keeper of photographs, tells me that many are blurred. A legacy of Amos's hours afloat alone with his ancient slow shutter camera in a boat that would not keep still.

Providing they did not get damp, glass negatives seem to have lasted much better than their modern equivalent, but they were very bulky to store and this led to many collections being destroyed. However, the negatives of the amateur photographer Thomas Naunton Waller (1863–1942), have been kept by his family. Waller grew up at Waldringfield, a peaceful Suffolk village on the River Deben. His father was the Rector, but they were never grand yachtsmen; simply had small boats in which they pottered about the river in the summer. T. Naunton Waller became a marine engineer and his skill with his hands led him to make his first camera in 1886.

This camera was a very simple affair and to expose the half-plate dry glass negative the leather cap was just removed from the lens. The early cameras were extremely unsophisticated and photography was not expensive. However, it was a long and tedious operation just to take one photograph. In the early days of photography the exposure of glass negatives was so slow that it was impossible to photograph boats afloat because they kept moving. The photographs of yachts and commercial ships in the mid-nineteenth century usually depicted them at low tide when they were firmly stationary on some harbour bottom.

Even in the 1880–90s the exposure time was still

very long and everyone had to keep still. This led the Victorians we see portrayed in photographs to appear more rigid and formal than they often were. Amateur photographers like T. Naunton Waller wanted to take relaxed family 'snap shots'. He found his home-made camera and its tripod too heavy for outdoor photography, so he bought a fold-up quarter plate camera, but in 1890 he resumed using his original camera and invented a mechanical shutter for it. The mechanism came largely from an old watch and preceded any reliable shutter on the market by several years.

T. Naunton Waller retired from his work on a Newcastle shipyard back to his native village. The family still live in Waldringfield, indeed the present Rector is the fourth generation of Wallers. It is this strong feeling of local identity with the Sandlings area of Suffolk that has led them to keep the Waller Collection. The photographs in the family album taken back in the 1880–90s have faded badly, but the glass negatives are still perfect apart from a few scratches.

An outstanding collection of family albums was compiled by Mrs R.J. Colman with her own photographs. She was the daughter of the shipowner Davies of Treborth, Anglesey, but the albums really began to be interesting when she married Russell James Colman, heir to the Colman Mustard fortune, and went to live in a large country house outside Norwich.

In the following photograph captions I have credited where possible the name of the photographer who, to the best of my knowledge, actually took the original photographs.

Handling the Gaff Yachts

2 Most of the crew of the schooner *Lyra* are aloft and about to ride down on the halliards in order to hoist the heavy gaff mainsail, 1883   (*West*)

3 ABOVE Mid-Victorian straight-stemmed racing cutter
Little Nell, 1884   (*West*)

5 RIGHT The schooner *Violet* and sloop yacht. Both
British yachts have single headsails like the American
schooner *America*, *c.*1868

4 ABOVE The cutter *Dolphin* at Swanage in September
1864 (*Col. Verschoyle*)

6 ABOVE The early clinker-hull cutter *Imp* in the Thames, *c*.1870 (*Unknown*)

8 BELOW Gaff rigged ice yacht on Windermere in the Great Freeze of 1895 (*Unknown*)

7 RIGHT Cruising yawl at the entrance of the River Ore, Suffolk, *c*.1875. A number of yachts built during this period were still sailing in 1976; these include the *Foam*, built by Pollard at Ilfracombe in 1876, *Sea Breeze*, 1873 and the Cowes oyster boat *Fanny*, 1872 (*Unknown*)

9   BELOW The New York schooner *Coronet*, built in 1885 in Brooklyn, has her topsail and outer jib stowed in a fresh breeze   (*Beken*)

10   RIGHT Two of the crew of the cutter *Deerhound* are on the bowsprit hanking the jib topsail on to the stay. *c*.1890   (*Beken*)

5384 *Coronet.*

DEERHOUND

11 BELOW Seventeen of the crew of *Valkyrie* are heaving up the running sail boom (*Beken*)

12 RIGHT *Ailsa* in the River Thames having a jackyard topsail set on 18 May 1895. Notice the mastheadman aloft (*West*)

13 German cutter *Meteor* close tacking with *Ailsa*,
August 1911. On the large gaff yachts a yard topsail or
club topsail had a single yard extending the sail above the
masthead. A jackyarder was a topsail with another yard
extending the sail past the gaff end.

14 *Shamrock II* after snapping her mast when racing on
22 May 1901   (*West*)

15 King Edward VII's racing cutter *Britannia*. Built in 1893 and designed by George Watson, then the leading British designer, the *Britannia* was a highly successful yacht and had extra magic because she belonged to the King. Men used to walk miles just to catch a glimpse of her racing (*Beken*)

15a The *Mariquita* and *Norada* astern. The *Mariquita*, built by Fife & Son, Fairlie in 1911, is one of the few yachts of this era to survive and in 1977 was a houseboat at Pin Mill, Suffolk (*Beken*)

Yachting Towns

16   Spectators at Cowes Week Regatta, *c*.1904   (*Beken*)

17 ABOVE Spectator yachts anchored off Cowes, *c.*1900
(*Beken*)

18 RIGHT *Satanita* and the American *Navahoe* racing at
Dartmouth, 1893 (*West*)

19 Steam yacht with some of the Regatta fleet at
Weymouth, 1901   (*Unknown*)

20   Dartmouth Harbour, 1898   (*Scott*)

22 RIGHT Gourock on the Clyde. The first Clyde Week was in 1877. Later the Clyde became popular as a base for cruising along the Highland coast (*Valentine*)

21 Yachts in Rothesay Bay

23 A Ramsgate trawler and a pleasure boat at Lowestoft, *c.*1905 (*Jenkins*)

24 Pleasure boats on Great Yarmouth beach, *c.*1894
(*Frith*)

25 BELOW Building the barge-yacht *Marietta* at
Woodbridge, 1915   (*Welton*)

26 Launching the *Marietta* at Woodbridge (*Welton*)

27 The *Rodney* awaits passengers on Aldeburgh beach,
*c.*1890 (*Frith*)

28, 29, 30   A series of Edwardian launches built by
Robertson at Woodbridge   (*Welton*)

Regatta Yachting

31 LEFT The *Bonnie Doon*, built by Fife & Son, Fairlie in 1867, racing at Harwich. Fife had a reputation for building particularly strong yachts, but some people claimed this made them too heavy for racing (*West*)

32 BELOW Victorian cutters and yawls off Felixstowe Dock, *c*.1880 (*West*)

33 The 1886 Harwich Regatta with the *Marjorie* and the white, steel hulled *Galatea* which had challenged the *Mayflower* for the America Cup the previous year (*West*)

34 Cutter *Bloodhound* with jackyard topsail set and a schooner racing, with a steam launch in the foreground, 1909 (*Beken*)

'BLOODHOUND' 1909

BEKEN
of Go

35 The clipper-bowed *Queen Mab* passing a straight-stemmed cutter. 1892 A racing rule introduced in 1882 resulted in the narrow, deep draught, Plank-on-edge type of hull evolving in Britain and in Continental yacht building   (*Beken*)

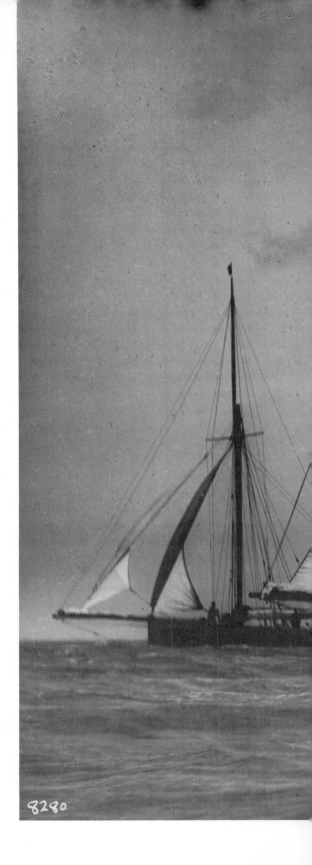

QUEEN MAB

Beken
of Cowes

SAMPHIRE

36 LEFT The elegance of a gaff yacht properly sailed is shown here in the *Samphire* (*Beken*)

37 ABOVE Master of the Menai Bridge cutter yacht *Aeolia*, 1895 (*Colman*)

38 BELOW Potter, Leavitt and Rice, crew of the Menai Bridge *Aeolia*, 1887 (*Colman*)

39 The Davies family on *Aeolia* in the Menai Straits, 1896   (*Colman*)

3663 "AILSA"   CANNES. MAR. 7. 95.   BRITANNIA

40 The *Ailsa* and the 83-foot *Britannia* racing off
Cannes, 7 March 1895 (*West*)

41 BELOW *L'Amoureuse* and *Eileen* carried six paid hands for racing, 1906 (*Beken*)

42 ABOVE The 52 Linear Rating *Sonya* leading her class
in The Solent. Most leading Edwardian racing yachts
had composite hulls of wooden planks on steel frames
(*Beken*)

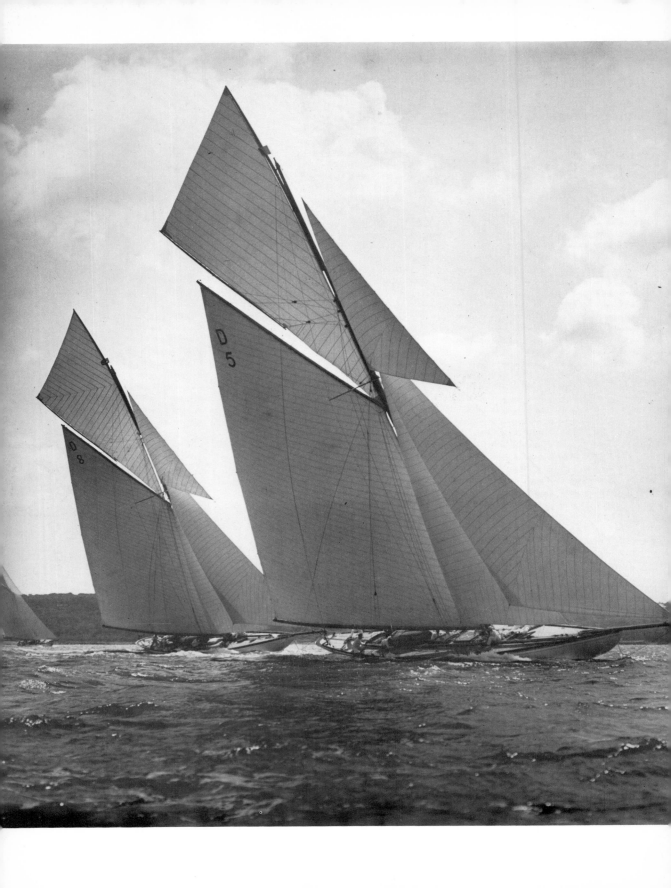

43 The Edwardian spoon-bowed racing cutters were
very much faster than the straight stemmed, counter
sterned Victorian cutters. c.1908   (*Beken*)

44 The start of the schooner class racing for the Brassey
Cup. *Adela, Meteor III, Germania* and *Cetoria*, 7 August
1908   (*Beken*)

45   The Spanish *Hispania* leading the 15-metre class,
1909   (*Beken*)

46   The American Herreshoff-design *Vigilant*. Defender
of the America Cup in 1896, the year which was virtually
the peak of large yacht racing. The American yachts were
beamy and shallow draught often with centreboards
(*Beken*)

47 The American *Columbia* crossing the finishing line to beat *Shamrock* for the third time and again retain the America Cup for that series. 1899 (*West*)

48 The Watson design *Valkyrie III*, 1895 (*West*)

49 The *Valkyrie III* was beaten by the American
Defender in the 1895 challenge (*West*)

Royalty Afloat

50 The *Alberta*, built 1863, was one of the smaller royal yachts and was used to ferry the Royal Family from Portsmouth to the Isle of Wight, 1898. The yacht was originally steered from a wheel aft   (*Beken*)

51   ABOVE The *Elfin* was built in 1849 as a tender to the
royal yachts. She was used to carry Queen Victoria's
letters to the mainland when she visited Osborne House
twice yearly   (*Beken*)

52 ABOVE King Edward VII, Queen Alexandra and their family aboard the Royal Yacht *Osborne*, 1880

53 LEFT King Edward VII on a yacht while visiting the Scilly Isles

54 Forecastle of the Royal Yacht *Victoria & Albert*.
Photograph taken by Queen Alexandra, *c.*1904

55 Felix Faure, sixth President of the Third Republic of
France and Czar Nicholas on the Russian Imperial Yacht.
This visit of Felix Faure put the seal on the
Franco–Russian Alliance. Note the deck has been
carpeted

56 The Czar of Russia's Royal Yacht *Standart*   (*Beken*)

57 Aboard *Britannia*. King Edward VII is talking to King
Alphonso of Spain. In the background the yachtmaster
is steering by using tiller lines   (*Beken*)

58 RIGHT The German Royal Yacht *Kaiser Adler*, 1892 (*Beken*)

59 BELOW The German Royal Yacht *Hohenzollern*, 1895 (*Beken*)

60 Kaiser Wilhelm II, second left, holding court on the German Royal Yacht *Hohenzollern* during a visit to Sweden, *c*.1910

61 Kaiser Wilhelm II, the German Emperor (*Beken*)

62 The Danish Royal Yacht *Dannebrog* coming alongside
Port Victoria Pier in the River Medway at the start of a
visit of the King and Queen of Denmark, 1914

Maritime Splendour

63 The 239-foot full-rigged ship, steam yacht *Valhalla* was owned by the Comte de Castellane of Le Havre. She was built by Ramage & Ferguson at Leith in 1892 (*Beken*)

64 BELOW The steam yacht *Amazon* owned by
Tankerville Chamberlayne   (*West*)

65 RIGHT Below on the *Brynhild*, 1908   (*Beken*)

66 On the *Soprano*, 1895   (*Beken*)

67 Crew of the *Soprano*, 1895 (*Beken*)

68 ABOVE Small steam yacht   (*Unknown*)

69 Cabin on the *Pampa*, 1907   (*Beken*)

70 ABOVE Rubicon's launch, standard pattern. Launches powered by internal combustion engines were rapidly replacing the steam launches. *c.*1912 (*Unknown*)

71 On the *Semiramis* (*Beken*)

Small Racing Craft

72   A group of South Coast l-raters racing, 1895   (*West*)

"Hoo Poo" 1892

73 The high peaked gunter mainsail racer *Hoo Poo*, 1892. This type of skimming dish replaced the plank-on-edge hull   (*Beken*)

74 The gunter rigged l-raters *White Rose* and *Whisper* in light airs off Portsmouth, 1895   (*West*)

75 BELOW The 'skimming dish' day racer *Kathleen*, c.1905 (*Beken*)

76 RIGHT Belfast Lough One Design, Class I, *Feltie* racing in Belfast Lough, 1898 (*Unknown*)

"KATHLEEN"

77 RIGHT The Dublin Bay 17-foot class *Hera* racing in 1905 with Ireland's Eye in the background. This class was started in 1898 as the Howth Sailing Club's one design and is the oldest keel boat class racing today in its original form   (*Unknown*)

78 ABOVE Dublin Bay 17 footers *Anita* and *Leila* on the Howth Sailing Club's starting line. These day racers are really miniature Victorian yachts complete with jackyard topsails

79 ABOVE, RIGHT By 1913 seventeen Dublin Bay One designs had been built. The original *Leila, Aura, Hera, Rita* and *Silver Moon* were built by Hilditch of Carrickfergus and sailed down to Howth. The introduction of one design classes gave a tremendous boost to small racing craft. Another survivor of early pioneering classes is the half rater Seabird. Started by the West Lancashire Yacht Club, Stockport in 1898, there were also fleets at Donaghadee, Gourock, Caernarvon and in the River Dee and the Mersey

80 RIGHT The Menai Straits l-rater class racing with the *Spindrift* leading, 1897 (*Colman*)

81 The open boats *Broadglance* and *Coot* raced by lady helmsmen, *c.*1910   (*Beken*)

82 A handicap fleet getting ready to race on the River Deben at Woodbridge. *c.*1913 (*Welton*)

83 BELOW Although one design classes were being established most Edwardian racing fleets were a mixed bunch, like these Woodbridge yachts which were raced on a handicap system, *c.*1910 (*Welton*)

84 BELOW, RIGHT The *Maid of Kent*, the victor in a three day match between England and Australia on the River Medway where she beat the *Irex* (*Eastmead*)

Cruising Yachts

85   The clipper bowed yawl *Silver Foam* built at Poole
in 1890 is fairly typical of small craft used for cruising.
She was based at Poole and carried two paid hands
(*Beken*)

86 The Workman family of Belfast chartered the
Petronilla in July 1912 for a cruise off the West coast of
Scotland. The yachting gear consists of no more than
John Workman's cap   (*Unknown*)

87 The paid crew of the *Petronilla* bending a jib-topsail in a loch on the West coast of Scotland, July 1912 (*Unknown*)

88 BELOW Cutter barge-yacht in the River Deben, *c*.1910 (*Welton*)

89 ABOVE Alan Colman at the tiller of *Chrone*, 1911

90 LEFT The fittings on *Chrone* show just how much craftsmanship and good material went into the building of the better Victorian yachts (*Colman*)

91   ABOVE Alan and Beryl Colman on the *Chrone* on passage from Lowestoft to Harwich, 1911   (*Colman*)

92   LEFT Owner of the small Gravesend yacht *Nellie*, *c*.1905   (*Unknown*)

94 ABOVE Edwardian clipper bowed gaff cutter *Myfanwy* in the Kyles of Bute   (*Macdonald*)

95 Because of the success of the Thames sailing barges in the Edwardian era many barge yachts like the *Apache* were built. *c*.1910   (*Beken*)

96 The barge yacht *Esnia* after launching from the Lime
Kiln Yard, Woodbridge, 1911   (*Welton*)

Inland Craft

97 A.P. Waller in a duck shooting punt at the River
Deben bar, 1889 (*Waller*)

98 ABOVE Fred Flegg and A.P. Waller in a lug sail boat
at Waldringfield, Suffolk, 1887 (*Waller*)

99 BELOW Launching of the Windermere racing cutter
Curlew, 1892 (*Unknown*)

100   ABOVE Fred, Joe and Jim, crew of the Norfolk
Broads hire yacht *Iantly*, 1893   (*Colman*)

101   BELOW Cabin of Norfolk Broads hire yacht *Iantly*,
August 1893   (*Colman*)

102 Holiday parties on Oulton Broad on a single headsail gaff yawl and a trading wherry which has a garden seat on the foredeck. 1897 (*Jenkins*)

103 Trading wherries, like this one at Lake Lothing, Lowestoft with a party of natty gents aboard, complete with banjo, used to have cabin tops fitted in the summer to accommodate holiday parties. *c*.1906   (*Jenkins*)

104 This Lowestoft gaff cutter yacht was probably
intended to sail at sea and on the Broads. 1895
(*Jenkins*)

105 These yachts all have the single headsails so unique
to the Broadland craft. *c*.1912 (*Jenkins*)

106 BELOW The *Castanet*, built by G. Mollett at Brundall in 1892, revolutionized Broadland racing. Previously yachts had followed the fashion of seagoing craft, but *Castanet's* 'skimming dish' hull led to the evolution of a type of inland yacht which flourished until 1914 (*Colman*)

107 RIGHT *Castanet's* owner R.J. Colman by the mast and his boatman Parker on the bow   (*Colman*)

108 ABOVE The Norfolk Dumpling class dinghies racing
in the Yare and Bure Regatta at Acle, Norfolk, 26 July
1909   (*Colman*)

109 RIGHT East Anglian Broadland was the only place
in the British Isle where a true type of inland
waterways yacht was evolved. This one is at Martham
Staithe on the River Thurne, *c*.1913   (*Jenkins*)

MARTHAM STAITHE.
. RIVER THURNE

110 Between the trees the Brown Boats (Broads 1 design) are seen racing on Oulton Broad, *c.*1906. Started in 1900 these are still racing regularly. This is a final glimpse into a long era when going afloat for pleasure had grown from the sport of a few to being much more widely spread. Yet most of the waterways, rivers and estuaries were unpolluted and as yet not overcrowded. This was a privileged golden age.